Music From The Romantic Era

Recital Pieces for
Violin & Piano

Spielstücke für Violine und Klavier

Grades Four to Seven

Edited with interpretative notes
by Elizabeth Turnbull

Herausgegeben mit kurzen Spielanweisungen von Elizabeth Turnbull

BOSWORTH

Music settings by Stave Origination
German translation by Dietmar Fratz
Series cover design by Miranda Harvey
Cover picture: *The Daughters of Catulle Mendes at the Piano*, 1888 by Pierre August Renoir (1841-1919)
Private Collection/Peter Willi/Bridgeman Art Library

ISMN: M-2016-4058-7

© 2000 Bosworth & Co. Ltd.
Published in Great Britain by Bosworth & Company Ltd.

Exclusive distributors:
Hal Leonard,
7777 West Bluemound Road,
Milwaukee, WI 53213
Email: info@halleonard.com

Hal Leonard Europe Limited,
42 Wigmore Street Maryleborne,
London, WIU 2 RY
Email: info@halleonardeurope.com

Hal Leonard Australia Pty. Ltd.
4 Lentara Court Cheltenham,
Victoria, 9132 Australia
Email: info@halleonard.com.au

Printed in EU

www.halleonard.com

CONTENTS

GYPSIES' MARCH	Oskar Rieding	2
PASTORALE	Oskar Rieding	8
ADORATION	Felix Borowski	13
BOLERO	Willem ten Have	17
RAGAMUFFIN	Joe Rixner	24
UN SOIR À PORTICI	Guido Papini	28
MIDNIGHT BELLS	R. Heuberger-F. Kreisler	37
SOUVENIR	František Drdla	42
MADRIGALE	František Drdla	47

RECITAL PIECES FOR VIOLIN & PIANO

GYPSIES' MARCH   Oskar Rieding   p. 2
First and third position
Take care to make a good even bow stroke in this piece. It should be played with short energetic strokes of the bow to give a good feeling of march rhythm.

PASTORALE   Oskar Rieding   p. 8
First and third positions
The bowing in the *moderato* must be evenly distributed and very smooth. Take care in the string crossings in the *più mosso*, keep the sound legato and the rhythm of the quavers very even.

ADORATION   Felix Borowski   p. 13
First to fifth positions
This melody needs to be played with an expressive legato use of the bow; it will also help you develop the ability to play with a sweet tone high on the A string.

BOLERO   Willem ten Have   p. 17
First, second and third positions with some chromatic fingering
This bolero needs a good full tone and a fluent shifting technique. It also makes good use of "shoeshine" bowing which must be light and melodic.

RAGAMUFFIN (Fiddle Polka)   Joe Rixner   p. 24
Mainly first to third positions with an optional run to seventh position
The bowing in this polka should be a light melodic spiccato not too short but riding easily slightly off the string as a "fiddler" would play. It will help develop good coordination between left and right hand in passages of fast notes.

UN SOIR À PORTICI (Tarantella)   Guido Papini   p. 28
First to fourth position
The bowing should be light and on the string. This piece has good use of fourth position and changes of position on the same note, which should be practised slowly for accuracy of intonation.

MIDNIGHT BELLS   Fritz Kreisler, after Richard Heuberger   p. 37
All positions
Take care that the separate bow quavers are smoothly played as part of the melodic line. They must not protrude dynamically. A good piece for increasing familiarity with the higher positions.

SOUVENIR   František Drdla   p. 42
Up to seventh position
This piece should be played as "salon" music, with a sweet tone and free rubato. The shifts and bowing in the first and last sections should be light and swift, whilst the middle section needs to be more intense and dramatic in colour.

MADRIGALE   František Drdla   p. 47
Up to fifth position
Madrigale should be played with a fluent melodic style and good use of rubato. Changes of position must be smooth and expressive.

Spielstücke für Violine und Klavier

ZIGEUNER-MARSCH   Oskar Rieding   S. 2
1. und 3. Lage
Achte in diesem Stück auf gleichmäßigen Bogenstrich. Kurze, energische Auf- und Abstriche sollen die Akzente für einen strengen Marschrhythmus setzen.

PASTORALE   Oskar Rieding   S. 8
1. und 3. Lage
Der Bogenstrich im *moderato* muss ausgeglichen und gefühlvoll sein. Achte auf die Saitenwechsel im *più mosso*, spiele alles legato mit exakten, gleichmäßigen Vierteln.

ANBETUNG   Felix Borowski   S. 13
1.-5. Lage
Diese Melodie erfordert ein ausdrucksstarkes legato; Das Stück schult das getragene, saubere Intonieren in hoher Lage auf der A-Saite.

BOLERO   Willem ten Have   S. 17
1.-3. Lage mit chromatischen Passagen
Dieser Bolero ist mit kräftigem, vollem Ton flüssig zu spielen. Die Leichtigkeit der Melodie darf unter dem ständigen Wechsel von Auf- und Abstrich nicht leiden.

SPITZBUB (Geigen-Polka)   Joe Rixner   S. 24
Vorwiegend 1.-3. Position mit möglicher Erweiterung bis in die 7. Lage
Die Bogentechnik bei dieser Polka soll hier zu leichtem, melodischem spiccato geführt werden, nicht zu abgehackt, aber rhythmisch federnd im "Fiddle"-Stil. Die Koordination zwischen linker und rechter Hand wird durch das Stück gefördert.

UN SOIR À PORTICI (Tarantella)   Guido Papini   S. 28
1.-4. Lage
Bei sachter Strichart wird hier der Wechsel von Saite und Lage bei gleichbleibendem Ton gefordert. Dies soll zuerst langsam und mit sauberer Intonation eingeübt werden.

MITTERNACHTSLÄUTEN   Fritz Kreisler nach Richard Heuberger   S. 37
Alle Lagen
Achte darauf, dass die Viertel auf neuem Bogen mit der Melodielinie verschmelzen. Kein Ton darf dynamisch aus der Rolle fallen. Eine gute Übung für das Spiel in höheren Lagen.

SOUVENIR   František Drdla   S. 42
Bis zur 7. Lage
Dieses Stück ist im Salonmusik-Stil mit weichem Ton und reichlich rubato zu musizieren. Rhythmus und Strichart im ersten und letzten Abschnitt sind leicht und locker auszugestalten, während der Mittelteil intensiv und dramatisch klingen soll.

MADRIGALE   František Drdla   S. 47
Bis zur 7. Lage
Das Madrigal soll stilecht mit flüssiger Melodie und ausgesuchtem rubato musiziert werden. Die Lagen sollen glatt und mit Ausdruck gewechselt werden.

Gypsies' March

Zigeuner-Marsch

(I. & III.)

OSKAR RIEDING
Op.23 No.2

Pastorale

(I. & III.)

OSKAR RIEDING
Op.23 No.2

Adoration
Anbetung
(I. - V.)

FELIX BOROWSKI

Bolero

(I. - III.)

WILLEM TEN HAVE
Op.11

24

Ragamuffin

Spitzbub

(I. - IV.)

JOE RIXNER
Arr. Leopold Beer

Un soir à Portici

Tarantella

(I. - IV.)

GUIDO PAPINI
Op.86

Midnight Bells
Mitternachtsläuten

Based on the melody of *Im Chambre Séparée* from *Der Opernball* by Richard Heuberger

FRITZ KREISLER

Souvenir

(I. - VII.)

FRANTIŠEK DRDLA

Madrigale

(I. - V.)

FRANTIŠEK DRDLA

✛ – ✛ optional cut